# BRICKS

# AND

# EXPERIMENTS

*BUILD CHALLENGES AND SCIENCE
EXPERIMENTS TO DAZZLE ANY
BRICK ENTHUSIAST*

Lindsay Whitman Drewes, M.A.

To David, William, and Mari, with love. Thank you for being perfect inspirations, scientists, and builders. You've taught me more than you'll ever know.
Love always,
Mom

Safety Note: Adult supervision and guidance are required for all activities in this book. Appropriate and reasonable caution is required at all times. The author of this book disclaims all liability for any damage, mishap, or injury that may occur while engaging in activities featured in this book.

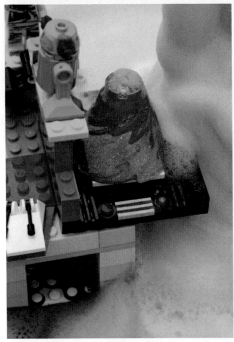

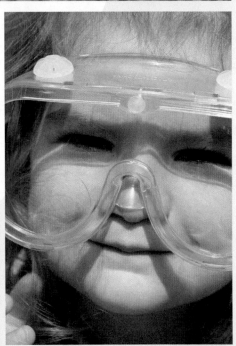

# TABLE OF CONTENTS

# INTRODUCTION

Welcome to the world of Bricks and Experiments, where build challenges and science experiments come together. This book is perfect for all ages and skill levels.

Each challenge can be modified to suit the youngest builders to the most seasoned builders. The beauty lies in the fun, creative aspect of building within your skill range while learning science, connecting with other builders, and trying something new.

There's no way to go wrong in these build challenges. Feel free to put your spin on each challenge and create something truly unique. Add levels of difficulty or simplify where needed.

The science experiments use simple, easy-to-find materials. All of the experiments require a helpful adult to oversee the steps for safety. The experiments lend a new way to experience brick building.

Whether you're a beginner or an expert, you'll find inspiration and ideas that will spark your imagination and get you building. It's time to grab your bricks and start experimenting!

ACTIVITIES

# BATTLE THE
# BLACK FIRE DRAGON

Travel to the pit of doom, where you'll meet the ever-growing black fire dragon. Prepare for battle by building a fortress and arming your most ferocious brick people with weapons. Set up the battle scene, then step back and watch as the fire dragon roars to life.

## BRICK CHALLENGE

This build challenge is to set up an epic battle scene. What brick warriors will you use to battle an ever-growing black fire dragon? What weapons, vehicles, or special equipment will they need to combat such a monster?

**Note:** A **real flame** will surround the fire dragon in this experiment. The dragon will be hot as it grows. **Brick People (and human people) should not actually fight the dragon.**

## MATERIALS

LIGHTER

3 TABLESPOONS OF SUGAR

1 TABLESPOON BAKING SODA

LIGHTER FLUID

FIREPROOF CONTAINER OR OUTDOOR STONE/CEMENT AREA

CERAMIC BOWL

SAND

6

# SCIENCE TIME

As the sugar burns next to the baking soda, it turns into black carbon or charcoal. The flame causes the baking soda to break down and release lots of carbon dioxide. The baking soda prevents the sugar from getting oxygen, forcing it into a charcoal form. It also pushes extra carbon dioxide gas right into the charcoal, trapping it. The trapped gas makes the charcoal lightweight. A combination of carbon dioxide gas and water causes the snake to grow upward.

# INSTRUCTIONS

- Add the sand to the bowl, then soak the sand with lighter fluid.

- Combine the baking soda and sugar, then pile the mixture onto the soaked sand surface.

- Light the sand with a long stick match or a long-neck lighter.

**NOTE:** The Fire Dragon will take about 10 minutes to form. Once it comes together, it will continue to grow as long as sugar and baking soda are still left.

**SAFETY NOTE:**
**KEEP SOME WATER NEARBY IN CASE YOU NEED TO EXTINGUISH THE FIRE.**

# Bricks and Experiments

Name :                     Date :

**Name of Today's Challenge :**

## Sketch

Sketch your build.

## Tell

Tell what happened during the experiment.

## Imagine

If you were to do this experiment and build challenge again, what would you change?

# THE FLOOR IS LAVA

Get ready! The floor is turning to lava! You must build something to save a brick person from a flowing stream of lava. Will your creation keep the brick person safe?

## MATERIALS

ASSORTMENT OF BRICKS

3 PLASTIC WATER BOTTLES

2 BOTTLES OF HYDROGEN PEROXIDE

1 TABLESPOON OF DRY YEAST

3 TABLESPOONS OF WARM WATER

LIQUID DISHWASHING SOAP

FOOD COLORING

MEDIUM-SIZE FUNNEL

SAFETY GOGGLES

## BRICK CHALLENGE

Build a platform, island, bridge, or any structure you think will keep a brick person safe from lava.

# INSTRUCTIONS

1. Once your builds are finished and positioned, place water bottles near the builds. If there is only one build, put all the bottles near it.
2. Mix the warm water and the yeast in a small cup for about 30 seconds. Make sure it has a consistency like melted ice cream. Add more warm water if needed.
3. Pour 1/2 cup of hydrogen peroxide liquid into each bottle using a funnel.
4. Add five drops of food coloring to each bottle.
5. Add 1 Tablespoon of liquid dish soap to each bottle and swish the bottle to mix it.
6. Pour the yeast and water mixture into the bottles with the funnel and watch the foam begin!
7. Once lava slows, your brick person has made it through the first level. Add another 1/2 cup of hydrogen peroxide to each bottle. Continue until lava reaches the brick person or hydrogen peroxide runs out. How many levels will your build survive?

## SCIENCE TIME

Hydrogen peroxide is made of hydrogen atoms and oxygen atoms. When the yeast comes into contact with hydrogen peroxide, it quickly breaks it down into water and oxygen. The dish soap traps the oxygen gas and produces the "lava flow" in this experiment.

SAFETY NOTE: **THE UNREACTED HYDROGEN PEROXIDE CAN IRRITATE SKIN AND EYES. MAKE SURE TO WEAR SAFETY GOGGLES WHILE EXPERIMENTING.**

# Bricks and Experiments

Name :                                          Date :

**Name of Today's Challenge :**

## Sketch

**Sketch your build.**

## Tell

**Tell what happened during the experiment.**

## Imagine

**If you were to do this experiment and build challenge again, what would you change?**

# MAGIC RAINBOW WITH LEPRECHAUN TREASURE ·····>

Get ready to capture a Leprechaun's treasure at the end of the rainbow. In this challenge, you'll have to build quickly so your brick person can find a way to reach the treasure. Finish your build before the rainbow is complete, or the leprechaun hides his treasure elsewhere.

## BRICK CHALLENGE

This brick experiment has two building challenges.

The first part of the challenge is to build a leprechaun's treasure that can float in the cup next to the paper towel rainbow. Make sure to add a brick treasure inside.

Once the treasure is created, the next challenge will be a race against time. Set up the experiment, then try to build a ladder, steps, or some way for a brick person to reach the treasure.

Make sure to finish the build before the two sides of the rainbow connect, or the leprechaun will take the prize.

## MATERIALS

ASSORTMENT OF RANDOM BRICK PIECES

PAPER TOWEL

WASHABLE MARKERS

WATER

2 SMALL GLASSES

# SCIENCE TIME

Paper towels are made from ground-up plant material. They are mostly cellulose, which is the material that forms plant cells. Water loves cellulose and is drawn to it.

In paper towels, there are lots of air pockets around the cellulose. The air pockets let more water flow to the cellulose.

In the paper towel rainbow, the water flows through the paper towel with the marker first, picking up the color. As the water flows through the air pockets to the cellulose, it takes the marker pigment with it, and the rainbow appears to grow.

# INSTRUCTIONS

1. Trim the paper towel to be 3 inches by 7 to 7.5 inches (shorter length means faster build challenge).
2. Make 1/2-inch rectangles using the colors of the rainbow at both ends of the paper towel.
3. Fill the cups 3/4 full of water. Put the paper towel in the cup so only the bottom edge touches the water.
4. The paper towel will absorb the water. As the water passes through the marker, the pigment will spread with the water to meet in the middle.
5. In about 10 minutes, the two sides of the rainbow will connect in the middle, signaling the end of the build challenge.

# Bricks and Experiments

**Name :**

**Date :**

**Name of Today's Challenge :**

## Sketch

**Sketch your build.**

## Tell

**Tell what happened during the experiment.**

## Imagine

**If you were to do this experiment and build challenge again, what would you change?**

# SAILBOAT RACES

Find a sea-worthy brick person and get ready to set sail!
Design the perfect sailboat to win the race with gusts of
wind powering your brick boat.

## MATERIALS

ASSORTMENT OF BRICKS

SAIL MATERIAL (BRICKS, PAPER, FABRIC,
ETC.)

CONTAINER OF WATER (9X13 INCH PAN,
BABY POOL, STORAGE CONTAINER, ETC.)

YARN

BOX FAN

## BRICK CHALLENGE

It's time to see who can
build the fastest sailboat!

Think about what qualities
make a quick boat. Get
creative and test along the
way.

In this build, the boat must
float evenly near the
water's surface and have a
sail (brick or otherwise)
that will catch the wind.

# INSTRUCTIONS

1. Design and build a sailboat! Have a container of water handy to test your build as you go along. Think about ways to make your boat float evenly and reduce its overall weight.
2. Stretch yarn across the water container to create lanes for all the boats racing.
3. Set the box fan at one end of the container of water.
4. Put the boats in position for the race and gently hold them in place until the race begins.
5. Count down to start the race and turn on the box fan. The first boat to reach the other side wins!
6. After the race, consider making design changes to create a faster boat.

## SCIENCE TIME

Want to make a boat that floats evenly on the water? It's all about buoyancy! Buoyancy is how well a material can float in water. Some materials are more buoyant than others based on their density. Density is how close the tiny pieces of the material are packed together. Different bricks or pieces can have different densities. Another critical factor is how the boat's weight is spread out over the water. The combination of density, weight, and how the weight is spread out will determine how buoyant the boat is.

16

# Bricks and Experiments

Name :                          Date :

**Name of Today's Challenge :**

## Sketch

**Sketch your build.**

## Tell

**Tell what happened during the experiment.**

## Imagine

**If you were to do this experiment and build challenge again, what would you change?**

# FIZZING GEM DIG

Treasure hunters, rejoice! This colorful, fizzy gem dig is a fun adventure. Get ready to mine your fortune with your favorite treasure-seeking brick person.

## BRICK CHALLENGE

Outfit a team of brick people treasure hunters. They will need tools to break into the "rock," treasure hunter outfits, and anything else you think will help the expedition.

Then, build a container to hold the treasures that will be unearthed.

## MATERIALS

ASSORTMENT OF BRICKS AND BRICK PEOPLE

DROPPER

VINEGAR

BAKING SODA

WATER

FOOD COLORING

SMALL TREASURES OR GEMS

BOWLS, SPOONS

LARGE CONTAINER TO HOLD EXPERIMENT

# SCIENCE TIME

A chemical reaction occurs when baking soda and vinegar come into contact. The fizzing you hear is carbon dioxide gas escaping from the reaction. If enough vinegar is used, the baking soda will completely break down and become carbon dioxide, water, and sodium acetate.

## INSTRUCTIONS

1. Add 2-3 cups of baking soda to a large bowl or container, using one bowl for each color of treasure rocks you wish to make.
2. Add several drops of food coloring to each bowl.
3. Slowly add the water and mix until reaching a doughy consistency. Too much water will make it difficult to form the balls.
4. Mold the baking soda dough into balls. Fold gems and treasures into each ball.
5. Put the baking soda balls into a container for the Fizzy Gem Dig.
6. Outfit a brick person as a treasure hunter to help with the dig.
7. Add a few drops of vinegar to the baking soda balls using a dropper to reveal the gems and treasures.

19

# Bricks and Experiments

Name :                    Date :

**Name of Today's Challenge :**

**Sketch your build.**

Sketch

**Tell what happened during the experiment.**

Tell

**If you were to do this experiment and build challenge again, what would you change?**

Imagine

# BRICK PEOPLE BOUNCY BALLS

The brick people of the future are preparing for a scientific mission in outer space. Together, they will leave Earth to study life on other planets. Each needs to be encapsulated in a space ball to bounce off Earth and into the cosmos. Get your team of scientist space adventurers together and prepare them for bounce-off.

## MATERIALS

BRICK PERSON

RUBBER GLOVES OR
DISPOSABLE GLOVES

1/2 CUP OF WARM WATER

1 TABLESPOON OF BORAX

BOTTLE OF CLEAR GLUE

GLITTER

## BRICK CHALLENGE

Choose your team of scientist space explorers. Dress them for the mission of exploring new worlds.

**NOTE:** BRICK PERSON CAN BE TAKEN OUT OF THE BOUNCY BALL AFTERWARD.

# INSTRUCTIONS

1. Stir 1/2 cup of warm water and 1 Tablespoon of Borax until completely dissolved.
2. Slowly pour about a Tablespoon of glue into the Borax solution. Once the glue interacts with the Borax, it will become gel-like.
3. Place brick person into the glue and add glitter.
4. Pour more glue on top until the glueball reaches the desired size.
5. Gently squeeze the glueball in the Borax solution until it is no longer sticky.
6. Remove from the Borax solution and roll it between your hands to shape it into a ball.

SAFETY NOTE: **BORAX CAN BE A SKIN IRRITANT, WEAR GLOVES AND KEEP OUT OF EYES. YOUNG CHILDREN SHOULD NOT HANDLE BORAX THEMSELVES.**

## SCIENCE TIME

Borax in water creates a link that holds the glue molecules together. This changes the glue from a liquid to a rubbery material called a polymer. A polymer is a special state of matter that can sometimes flow like a liquid and sometimes act like a solid.

# Bricks and Experiments

Name :                                    Date :

Name of Today's Challenge :

**Sketch**

Sketch your build.

**Tell**

Tell what happened during the experiment.

**Imagine**

If you were to do this experiment and build challenge again, what would you change?

# UNDERWATER RAINBOW RAIN

It's time to go underwater for this experiment. Create an underwater scene and watch as rainbow rain falls around your scuba diving brick people.

## BRICK CHALLENGE

Underwater builds can be particularly challenging because most of the bricks will float. Get creative and build something you'd like to see underwater.

Advanced builders can try to make a heavy enough build to stay at the bottom of the container.

Beginning builders can use rocks to help their creations remain underwater.

## MATERIALS

ASSORTMENT OF BRICKS

FOAMING SHAVING CREAM

FOOD COLORING

CLEAR CONTAINER WITH WATER

GRAVEL OR FISH TANK STONES

24

# INSTRUCTIONS

1. Construct an underwater build. Submerge creation in water. Weigh down with rocks, if needed.
2. Cover the top of the water with foaming shaving cream.
3. Add drops of food coloring to the shaving cream in different locations to create a variety of rainbow colors.
4. Watch the colorful show!

# SCIENCE TIME

Clouds are made up of tiny water droplets and bits of dust in the air. Inside the cloud, the water droplets come together and form bigger droplets.

When these droplets become too big to stay in the air, they fall to the Earth as rain.

In this experiment, the food coloring droplets are too big for the shaving cream clouds to hold, so they fall from the cloud as a colorful "rain."

# Bricks and Experiments

**Name :**  **Date :**

**Name of Today's Challenge :**

## Sketch

Sketch your build.

## Tell

Tell what happened during the experiment.

## Imagine

If you were to do this experiment and build challenge again, what would you change?

# BRICKS AND CRYSTAL ART

The people of Bricktopia have decided to beautify their city and chose YOU as the artist for the job. Can you design brick structures with hanging crystal art inside? The citizens want to place these sculptures along bike paths and in parks for everyone to enjoy.

## MATERIALS

CRAFT PIPE CLEANERS

MEDIUM SIZE CONTAINER

STRING

PENCIL OR CRAFT STICK

BORAX

WATER

## BRICK CHALLENGE

Design a brick structure that can stand while having a piece of crystal art hanging from it. Think of unique ways to bring together the brick structure and crystal pieces. Get inspiration from outdoor sculptures online or in your community.

# SCIENCE TIME

Hot water can dissolve more Borax than cool water. As the water cools, Borax begins to fall out of the solution because the water can't hold as much. The Borax sticks to rough surfaces like pipe cleaners and forms crystal seeds. As more Borax comes out of the solution, it arranges itself in specific and repeated patterns around the seeds, forming crystals.

## INSTRUCTIONS

1. Bend, twist, cut, and combine pipe cleaners to form a shape or design.
2. Find a container that is large enough for the pipe cleaner design to be completely submerged.
3. Decide how many cups of water you will need to cover the creation.
4. Tie a piece of string to the pipe cleaner design and tie the other end to a pencil or craft stick.
5. Suspend the pipe cleaner design in the container by resting the pencil or craft stick across the top of the container and letting the design hang below. The pipe cleaner design should not touch the bottom of the container.
6. Begin heating water in the pot on high.
7. When the water is boiling, add 1 Tablespoon of Borax per cup of water.
8. Stir until the Borax dissolves in the water.
9. Let the solution cool for a few minutes, then pour it into the container.
10. Let it set for 1-4 days. Crystals will form within 24 hours, but the longer it sits, the more crystals can form.

# Bricks and Experiments

**Name :**                    **Date :**

**Name of Today's Challenge :**

## Sketch

**Sketch your build.**

## Tell

**Tell what happened during the experiment.**

## Imagine

**If you were to do this experiment and build challenge again, what would you change?**

# MAGIC POTION

······································▶

A wizard has made a magic potion that reveals a challenge when mixed with other liquids. Build something that matches the color of the potion, or the wizard might cast a spell on you!

## BRICK CHALLENGE

Create a build using only one color or different shades of that color.

Can you make a build that matches each magic potion created by the wizard?

## MATERIALS

A SMALL RED CABBAGE, GRATED

POT OF BOILING WATER

STRAINER

TWO LARGE BOWLS

SMALL CUPS

SAFETY GOGGLES

LEMON OR LIME JUICE

VINEGAR

BLEACH

SPRITE

1/2 CUP WATER WITH 1 TABLESPOON

BAKING SODA DISSOLVED

AMMONIA

30

# SCIENCE TIME

Red cabbage is reddish-purple because of a pigment called anthocyanin. This pigment is also in blueberries, grapes, and purple flowers.

In different solutions, anthocyanin interacts with the molecules and changes colors.

In acidic solutions, the pigment turns red. In neutral solutions, it turns purple. And in basic solutions, it turns blue, green, or yellow. This makes red cabbage an excellent indicator for testing the pH of different liquids.

# INSTRUCTIONS

1. Grate a small red cabbage and put it into a bowl.
2. Cover the cabbage with boiling water.
3. Let the cabbage steep until the water is at room temperature. The water should be purple.
4. Strain the cabbage water into a bowl.
5. Fill small cups each with baking soda water, Sprite, bleach, vinegar, ammonia, lemon, or lime juice. *Note: keep the liquids in these cups separate.
6. Get ready for the wizard to do his magic. Pour a little of the cabbage water into each cup and watch as the color changes.
7. Create single-color builds to match the magic solutions.

# Bricks and Experiments

**Name :**                    **Date :**

**Name of Today's Challenge :**

## Sketch

**Sketch your build.**

## Tell

**Tell what happened during the experiment.**

## Imagine

**If you were to do this experiment and build challenge again, what would you change?**

# SPELLBINDING EGGS

In a magical land, enchanting brick people hatch from beautiful and unique crystal eggs. Each egg color grants them different extraordinary powers. Grow crystal eggs and build a world where your brick friends will hatch from the eggs and gain magical abilities.

## MATERIALS

BORAX

SCHOOL GLUE

FOOD COLORING

4-5 EGGS

SCISSORS

PAINTBRUSH

LATEX GLOVES

CUPS OR CONTAINERS

WATER

NAPKINS

## BRICK CHALLENGE

Create an enchanted world where you can find these special eggs. Use your imagination to come up with stories about what magical powers each egg color might give to the brick creatures that hatch from them. Have fun, and let your creativity flow as you build your new world.

33

# INSTRUCTIONS

1. Crack the eggshell in half lengthwise and cut it in half with scissors.
2. Using a small paintbrush, coat the inside surface of each half with a thin layer of glue.
3. Pour 1 cup of Borax into a small bowl. Using glove-covered hands, put the glue-covered eggshell into the bowl and cover with Borax. Set aside to dry.
4. Combine 3 cups of water and 1 1/4 cups of Borax. Heat until the Borax dissolves.
5. Put 5-10 drops of food coloring into each cup or container. Fill each cup or container with enough slightly cooled Borax solution to cover the egg.
6. Submerge the eggshells into the solution with the cut edges facing up.
7. Set containers in a place where they won't be disturbed. The crystals will begin to form within a couple of hours. The longer the eggs sit, the larger the crystals will grow. Leave for 4-7 days for best results.
8. Remove the eggshells from the cups and set them on napkins to dry.
9. Add brick friends to the shells and create a fantastic story.

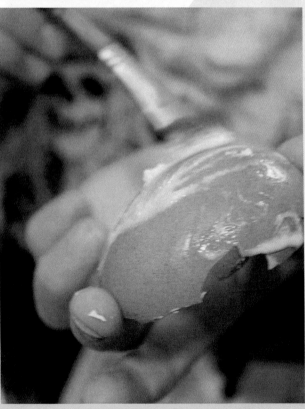

# SCIENCE TIME

Like in the Bricks and Crystals Art experiment, when the water is heated, it can hold more Borax, creating a supersaturated solution. The eggshell's smooth surface allows the Borax glued onto it to form seed crystals. As the water cools, the Borax falls out of the water and arranges itself into a specific, repeated pattern around the seeds. This pattern forms the crystals.

# Bricks and Experiments

Name :                          Date :

Name of Today's Challenge :

## Sketch

Sketch your build.

## Tell

Tell what happened during the experiment.

## Imagine

If you were to do this experiment and build challenge again, what would you change?

# BRICK
# BUILDING
# CHALLENGE
# CARDS

Build a bridge and test how much weight it can hold.

Build a picture frame and add a photo or drawing to it.

Build the floor plan to the ultimate clubhouse.

Build a house.

Make a 2D picture or mosaic.

Make an insect.

Make a piece of playground equipment.

Make a piece of food.

Create something using only bricks of one color.

Make a monochromatic build - use black and white bricks and only one other color.

Make a tower. How tall can you make it?

Make a catapult.

Make a food truck. What type of food does it sell?

Make a monument. Who or what does it honor?

Make a trophy. What does someone have to do to win it?

Create a magic key. What does it unlock?

Build a birdhouse.

Create an item from a book; a magic wand, a poison apple, a flying car, or anything you've read about lately.

Make a
rainbow.

Make a
marble
maze.

Build
a
flower.

Make
a
pizza.

Pretend
you're in a
plane and
build a farm
you would
see from the
sky.

Build a
snowflake,
leaf, sun, or
tulip,
depending
on what
season it is.

IDEA TIME

Use this space to sketch and plan new builds and experiments.

Use this space to sketch and plan new
builds and experiments.

Use this space to sketch and plan new builds and experiments.

STUD ART

Most brick builds are three-dimensional (3D). To create Stud Art, you'll work with two-dimensional (2D) creations on paper.

Switching from creating in 3D to creating in 2D can be mind-bending!

Use a marker to connect the studs on the following pages one line at a time to create 2D brick art.

For a free PDF printable of additional Stud Art Pages, visit www.LindsayWD.com.

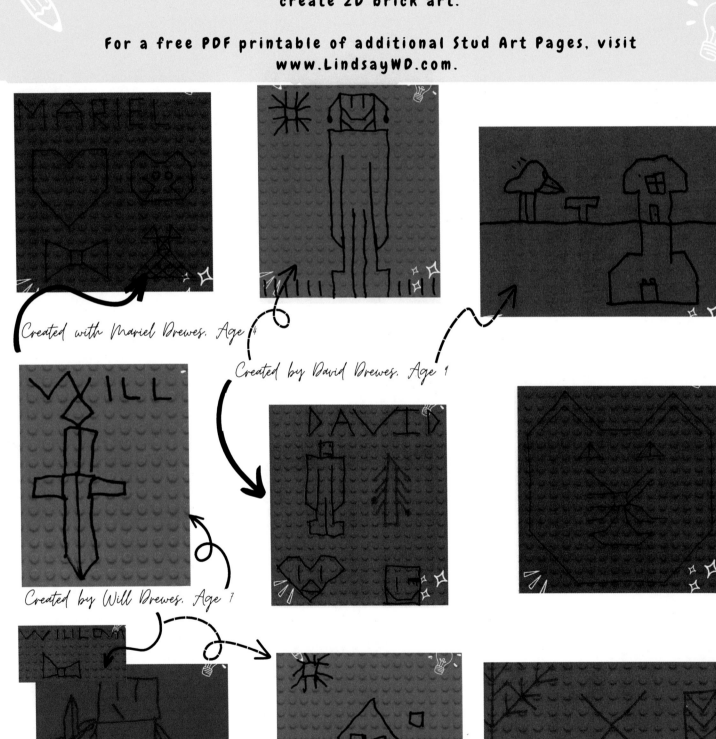

Created with Mariel Drewes, Age 4

Created by David Drewes, Age 1

Created by Will Drewes, Age 7

Connect the studs one line at a time to create 2D brick art.

# Connect the studs one line at a time to create 2D brick art.

# Connect the studs one line at a time to create 2D brick art.

# Connect the studs one line at a time to create 2D brick art.

Connect the studs one line at a time to create 2D brick art.

Made in the USA
Las Vegas, NV
14 January 2024